For Robert Dodd. E.D.

This paperback edition published in 2003
First published in Great Britain in 1999 by Zero To Ten Limited,
part of the Evans Publishing Group
2a Portman Mansions
Chiltern Street
London W1U 6NR

British Library Cataloguing in Publication Data
Reidy, Hannah
    All sorts of noises
    1. Sound - Pictorial Works - Juvenile literature
    I. Title
    534

ISBN 1-84089-287-0

Printed in Hong Kong

ALL
SORTS of
Noises

Written by Hannah Reidy
Illustrated by Emma Dodd

Bbring!

Groan!

Tweet!
Tweet!

Before her eyes are
even open, Evie can hear

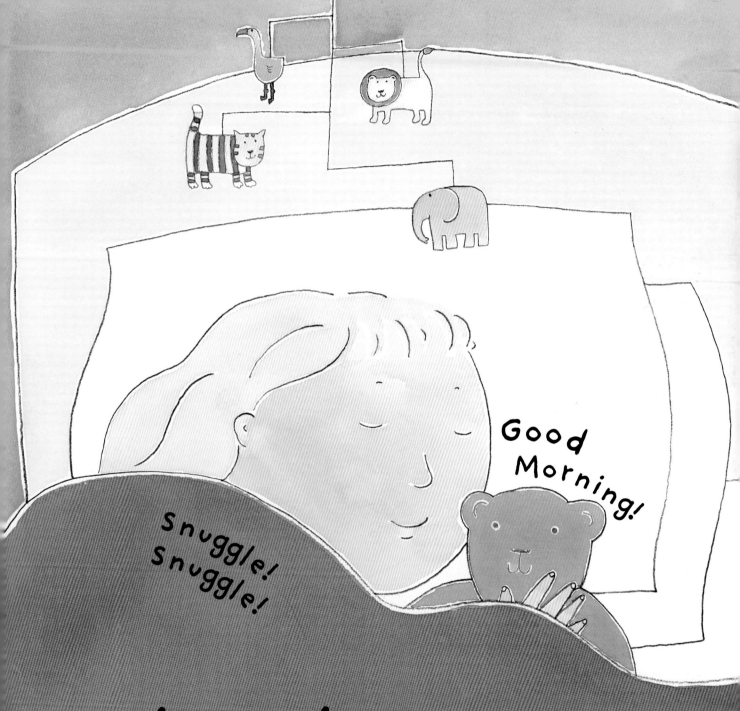

morning noises.

Between bites of her breakfast,
Kesia can just about hear

kitchen noises.

Holding Dad's hand
all the way, Stuart can hear

street noises.

Brenda can hear playgroup noises.

Hugh can hear people noises.

Aachoo!

Aachoo!

Doctor

Lying in the green,
green grass
Rosie can hear

garden noises.

As her silly sister splashes Dad, Beth can hear **bath-time noises.**

Tired and tucked up tight,
Nina can hear

What noises do

these things make?